LEGO
THE NINJAGO MOVIE
THE ESSENTIAL GUIDE
WRITTEN BY JULIA MARCH

CONTENTS

Introduction	6
Ninjago City	8
Lord Garmadon	10
Shark Army	12
Secret Ninja Force	14
Lloyd Garmadon	16
Lloyd's Mech Dragon	18
Lloyd's Home	20
Nya	22
So Ninja!	24
Popular Opinion	26
Jay	28
Noticeboard	30
Volcano Lair	32
General #1	34
Garma Mecha Man	36
Master Wu	38
Warring Wisdom	40
Destiny's Bounty	42
Cole	44
My Secret Diary	46
City Battle	48
Kai	50
Perilous Journey	52
The Jungle	54
Zane	56
Temple	58
Lessons from the Jungle	60

AN INTRODUCTION

By Master Wu

Imagine a city. A beautiful city, where citizens begin every day by singing. Ninjago City!

Now imagine that city attacked by a nasty villain, again and again. Imagine a battle between father and son, between good and evil.

Only the lessons of a wise ninja master can bring peace to this troubled place. But will my pupils – the Secret Ninja Force – learn those lessons in time?

Step into Ninjago City to find out. Oh, and if you see the villain and his fearsome army, remember to run!

AN INTRODUCTION

By Lord Garmadon

Imagine a city. A beautiful city, where citizens begin every day by screaming. Ninjago City!

Now imagine that city waiting to be conquered by a super-awesome, all-powerful leader, again and again. Imagine a battle between two, unrelated individuals, between a warlord and a ninja.

Only the lessons of an old flute player can spoil this excellent plan. Hopefully his pupils – the Secret Ninja Force – won't be smart enough to learn those lessons in time.

Join the fearsome Shark Army and invade Ninjago City to find out. Get a move on!

NINJAGO CITY

Ninjago City is bustling, vibrant and prosperous, yet there's something unusual about it, too. There's always lots of construction going on, but the city never grows beyond its limits. It's like the citizens are just rebuilding the same structures over and over again.

Pufferfish blimp is home to a floating sushi restaurant.

Top visitor attractions

The beach
It is very safe to swim here. No sharks have been spotted – yet.

Restaurants
Cuisines from all over the world can be enjoyed here.

Skyscrapers
For the best view, head for the highest floor of the tallest tower. The tallest one this week, that is!

Golden sands and softly lapping waters.

Watery world

Down at the lowest levels of the city, boats bob in the docks or glide along waterways. This is the oldest part of Ninjago City, where many traditional ways of life and older buildings can be found.

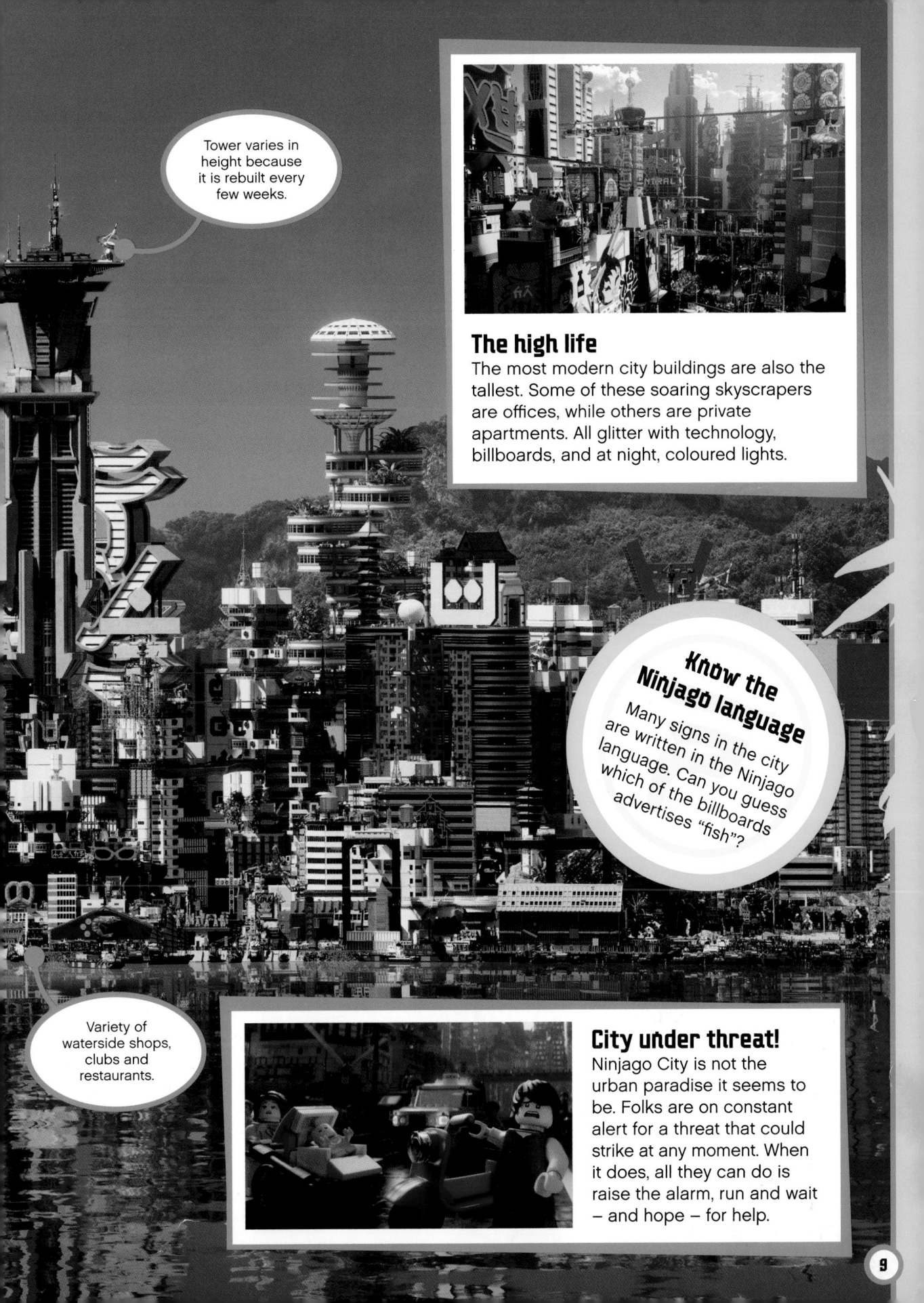

Tower varies in height because it is rebuilt every few weeks.

The high life

The most modern city buildings are also the tallest. Some of these soaring skyscrapers are offices, while others are private apartments. All glitter with technology, billboards, and at night, coloured lights.

Know the Ninjago language

Many signs in the city are written in the Ninjago language. Can you guess which of the billboards advertises "fish"?

Variety of waterside shops, clubs and restaurants.

City under threat!

Ninjago City is not the urban paradise it seems to be. Folks are on constant alert for a threat that could strike at any moment. When it does, all they can do is raise the alarm, run and wait – and hope – for help.

LORD GARMADON

If he can't rule the city, he'll destroy it

This cruel conqueror is feared by all in Ninjago City. It's because he keeps returning to destroy the place... over and over again. Citizens call Lord Garmadon "The Worst Guy Ever", but only when he is safely out of earshot.

Did you know?

Lord Garmadon has had many elaborate plots to take over the city in the past. He has led troops of Insect Warriors, Bird Soldiers and even a Fruit Army.

Best dressed worst guy

Lord Garmadon has four arms, red eyes and a smile that could sour milk. He also has a relentless drive to crush the Ninjago people (and to crush their city). A guy this bad must dress to oppress, in dark robes and a towering horned helmet.

His helmet makes Lord Garmadon look taller than he is.

Nerds look a little nervous around their bad-tempered boss.

Garmadon's nerds

Garmadon has surrounded himself with a team of IT nerds who labour in his lab night and day. They create the scientific gadgets, weapons and mechs Garmadon hopes will give him the edge in his next battle with the ninja.

Shark staff is tipped with a blade bearing tooth-like spikes.

Garmadon's life goals

Rule Ninjago City
When he finally has control, he might stop smashing up the city. Might.

Defeat the Secret Ninja Force
So far, they've been very, very lucky.

Bond with Lloyd, his long-lost son
Lloyd will have to turn evil first. Then – Garmadons united!

Garmadon likes clothes in dark colours. They go with his mood.

Don't talk back!

Few of Lord Garmadon's soldiers dare to disobey his orders. Complete obedience is expected – and complete silence too, so that Garmadon can enjoy the sound of his own voice shouting commands.

SHARK ARMY

Lord Garmadon is back in Ninjago City with a fishy new fighting force – his Shark Army! With sea-creature armour and vehicles to match, they bring chaos to the city. Chaos, but not necessarily victory, much to Garmadon's disgust.

Brown Beanie guy

Strength: Easily blends in with ordinary citizens.
Weakness: No armour makes him vulnerable to attack.

Octopus

Strength: Able to wield several weapons at once.
Weakness: Sometimes gets tangled in his own tentacles.

Hammerhead shark

Strength: Wide-angle vision device in helmet.
Weakness: Bulbous eyes are weak spots.

Jellyfish

Strength: Clear-headed, with 360-degree range of vision.
Weakness: Bad team player, lives in his own little bubble.

Pufferfish

Strength: Huge helmet to intimidate enemies.
Weakness: Easily deflated when foes don't back down.

Great white shark

Strengths: Swift, ruthless and super, super aggressive.
Weakness: Rushes in before orders given, ruining attacks.

Lobster

Strengths: A shifty sidestep and powerful pinches.
Weakness: Crabby; wastes time squabbling with allies.

Anglerfish

Strength: Won't let a foe off the hook once caught.
Weakness: Fixating on one foe allows others to escape.

Manta Ray Bomber

This flyer swoops low to release its bombs. If it crashes in the sea, the pilot escapes in the cockpit boat.

Mobile Crab

The crab vehicle pilot controls a huge pincer with one hand and a shooter with the other. He aims to leave the ninja shell-shocked.

Flying Jelly Sub

Twisting tentacles dangle from this sub when it is airborne. After landing, it scuttles and spins on its rotating legs.

SECRET NINJA FORCE

Every time Lord Garmadon attacks Ninjago City, a mysterious band of ninja appears. The ninja fight him off with their amazing skills, weapons and mechs. The citizens don't know where these six city saviours come from. They don't really care. They are just glad they come!

White Ninja
Witnesses have said there's something slightly odd – even a little robotic – about the ninja in the ice-white costume.

Silver Ninja
This ninja goes with the flow. One moment she's as silent as a shadow, the next she's a spinning, spear-wielding warrior.

Green Ninja
The ninja in the green robes seems to be the leader – the others often gather around him. Folks who have seen him have noted his serious expression.

Black Ninja

The feats of strength this ninja can perform are incredible. He shows off his muscles with his sleeveless, dark ninja robes.

Red Ninja

This ninja is a fiery character all right! In fact, he fights with such intensity that he can sometimes seem a little scary, even to people he is trying to help!

Blue Ninja

This ninja has been described as "fast as lightning". After a battle, he is usually the first to lighten the mood with a joke or a funny dance.

LLOYD GARMADON

Secret ninja leader shamed by his name

Life is hard for Lloyd. His villainous dad, Lord Garmadon, left when Lloyd was just a baby. Now, the whole city holds his evil father against him. It is enough to send the average teenager into a sulk. But not Lloyd. He's a ninja and he has a city to save!

All you need is Mum

Lloyd is close to his mum, Koko. She's done a great job of bringing him up alone. Lloyd wishes he could let her into the secret that he is the Green Ninja. Little does he know that Koko has a secret of her own!

Hood helps block out the sound of his classmates' jokes.

Lloyd has grown quick on his feet to avoid being noticed.

The Green Ninja's signature weapon is a sharp sword.

Lloyd's family tree

Lord Garmadon
Lloyd's absent father is really evil. Maybe it's just as well he stays away.

Koko
Lloyd has a warm, loving mum, but she doesn't like talking about his dad.

Master Wu
His elderly uncle and teacher is sometimes a little too mysterious.

Unpopular with the population

It's not Lloyd's fault his dad is the Worst Guy Ever, but people hold it against him anyway. It's bad enough when his classmates boo him, without his teachers joining in too. No wonder Lloyd likes to hide behind a hood.

The Green Ninja

Lloyd is the Green Ninja – leader of the Secret Ninja Force. Lloyd isn't sure why Master Wu chose him as leader, but he takes his role very seriously. He wears his green-trimmed robes with pride, and spends hours at sword practice.

LLOYD'S MECH DRAGON

The ninja think technology is the key to beating Lord Garmadon. If they keep making better mechs than his, they will surely win in the end. Master Builder Lloyd builds all their vehicles. None is more awesome than his own mean, green dragon machine! The Dragon Mech soars through the Ninjago skies, racing to save the day.

Lloyd in control

It takes skill to fly a mech of this size. Lloyd sits at the controls in the cockpit. He operates the dragon's jaws, tail and weapons while controlling its speed and altitude. With Wu looking on, he doesn't want to make a mistake.

Snapping jaws open and close to grab enemies.

Spiked, swooshing tail is operated by turning a wheel.

All limbs are fully jointed and move independently.

Each foot bears two sharp, golden claws.

Know the Ninjago language

The dragon gives clues to the Green Ninja's true identity with symbols for "L" and "Lloyd" on its sides.

Moving machine

The dragon is made up of jointed segments so it can easily twist, turn and arch as it flies. Enemy vehicles are no obstacle for this flexible beast.

Beware the dragon

Most foes are transfixed by the mech's snapping jaws. They rarely notice the missiles on its legs until it's too late. And when the pop-out thrusters fire, the dragon will be on top of them before they know it!

LLOYD'S HOME

In central Ninjago City, space is hard to come by. Most people live in small flats in commercial blocks. In Lloyd and Koko's block, the lower floors bustle with shops, banks, cafés, bars, markets and leisure facilities.

Did you know?

To get from the bottom level to the top level of Lloyd's block, you can take the lift or phone for a flying taxi.

Home... alone

Living at home with Mum does not mean that Lloyd never gets lonely. Everyone apart from his ninja friends rejects him – and that hurts. It's all his dad's fault! Lying in bed at night, Lloyd wishes his dad could be good.

Sushi break

Lloyd and Kai have treated themselves to a sushi break at a local eatery. They're looking forward to an hour of chilling, chatting and tasty snacks. Let's hope Garmadon doesn't choose this moment to attack!

NYA

The best at being the best

Nya is not just a brilliant fighter and a quick thinker, she's a great motivator too. Rallying the team is one of her finest skills. In fact, it's hard to think of something Nya isn't good at. At least that is what she is quick to tell her brother and fellow ninja, Kai.

Nya vs Kai arguments

Which is better – fire or water?
Nya knows water can put out Kai's flames in no time!

Who has more fans in the city?
Clearly Silver Ninja fans outnumber Red Ninja fans.

Who is the most humble?
Nya is the best at being humble. She's best at everything.

Always on duty

When Nya isn't being a ninja, she dresses down in casual street clothes. But she is still ready to leap into action if there is trouble in Ninjago City. When a police rickshaw gives chase to a villain, Nya hops aboard to lend a little secret ninja muscle.

Watertight cockpit can rotate around 360 degrees.

Hoverpad-style feet enable the Strider to climb buildings.

Nya's Water Strider

In her bug-like Water Strider, Nya takes any battle in her stride. It walks on water or on land, and can even climb walls. Nya can rotate the cockpit to keep the enemy in sight, then take aim and release a missile from the six-stud rapid shooter. Bullseye!

Long, jointed legs move independently of each other.

Water warrior

Nya makes sure foes get the point when she goes after them with her mighty spear! Nya's silver Secret Ninja Force armour features an overskirt made of tough, studded fabric to protect her upper legs in battle.

SO NINJA!

After each victory, the ninja celebrate by shouting that they are "so ninja!" They put their success down to their mechs. These high-tech machines are awesome, but they aren't the only thing the ninja need to defeat Garmadon.

Secret store

It is essential to store the mechs away from prying, non-ninja eyes. An old warehouse by Ninjago City docks is the ideal place. The roof opens for access from above.

What makes a mech?

A mech is a robotic machine that is worn or driven. When operated with skill, it almost becomes a part of its owner. Lloyd has built each ninja a custom mech that reflects their personality.

The ice powers of Zane's mech will

Cole manoeuvres his mech into tight spots with ease.

Full force

The mechs are great at defeating enemies. The city's citizens are so grateful to the ninja that they don't mind clearing up the mess left behind. After all, the people of Ninjago City will always rebuild!

Enemies get a shock when caught by a lightning bolt from Jay's mech.

When things heat up in battle, Kai's mech is never far away.

Lloyd's Dragon Mech is a welcome sight for

Skilful Nya pilots her Strider through the narrow streets and canals of the city.

POPULAR OPINION

Ninjago City buzzes with songs and stories about the Secret Ninja Force. Their leader, the Green Ninja, is the most popular guy in town. Nobody knows he is really Lloyd Garmadon – the most unpopular guy in town!

Everyone's gone green!

All the ninja have their fans, but the Green Ninja is by far the most popular. He is often the one to deal the final blow that defeats Lord Garmadon. If only he would get rid of Lloyd Garmadon, too!

Nobody loves Lloyd

The people of Ninjago City are a friendly bunch – except to Lloyd. Who wants to be friends with a guy whose dad ruins *everything*? People decide it is best not to talk to Lloyd, just to be on the safe side.

JAY

He has the skills but he needs to chill

Jay appears chatty and outgoing, but secretly he is filled with doubts. What if his ninja skills aren't up to scratch? When this nervous ninja isn't stressing about that, he's stressing about something else – his admiration for Nya.

Ready in a flash

As the Ninja of Lightning, Jay wears a robe trimmed with electric blue. His orange scarf and leg bindings add striking pops of colour. Hours of practice in the dojo have made Jay an expert with his hefty spiked flail.

Knee straps give extra support for high ninja kicks.

Know the Ninjago language

Hidden beneath Jay's cross-body belt are the Ninjago language characters for "spark". Perfect for the Ninja of Lightning!

Jay's Lightning Jet

Bolts of lightning crackle in the sky over Ninjago City. It isn't an electrical storm – it's Jay in his Lightning Jet! This amazing craft has a whirling electro disc to generate energy. Lots of antennae divert the energy at foes. Now that's what you call a bolt from the blue!

Rotating electro disc generates power.

Jay sits in dome-shaped cockpit.

Antennae deliver a shocking blast.

Happy families

Jay is happy that his parents, Ed and Edna, aren't villains like Lloyd's dad is. They are supportive of everything Jay does, even if it is making brave fashion choices like his orange scarf.

Jay's signature weapon is a silver flail.

Jay's biggest worries

Letting his teammates down
He fears making an error that will cost the ninja a victory.

Upsetting Nya
He would be utterly crushed if his crush crushed his hopes.

People finding out about Edna's seashell collection
Not cool, Mum! (They are kind of pretty though...)

NOTICEBOARD

At Ninjago High School, everyone knows where to go to find out the latest news. The school noticeboard is constantly updated with rules, messages, awards, reminders and sometimes warnings. Not all of them are placed there by the staff!

FOUND
A green scarf-type thing with a funny symbol on it. Looks a bit like a ninja hood... Collect from the principal's office.

You're the best, Green Ninja!

New menu this week in the school canteen!

Join us for meals inspired by recent events in Ninjago City.

No food fights, please!

- Ninja noodles
- Saucy sharkburgers
- Mecharoni cheese

What to do in an emergency!

Please remember these procedures in times of city attack.

- Always stick together to stay safe.
- Listen to your teachers at all times.
- Remain in your classroom. Get a hall pass if you and your friends need to leave mysteriously.
- No bullying of anyone at any time. Even if their father is the evil villain destroying the city.

Jay ♥ Nya

DON'T FORGET CAREERS DAY NEXT WEEK!

Remember, Friday is **Bring Your Parent to School Day**. We want to hear from your mums and dads about what it's like to be a firefighter, a builder or a barista in Ninjago City.

P.S. If your last name is Garmadon, DON'T bring your dad to school.

Sponsored by the Master Re-Builders' Association.

TALKS FROM:

Local fisherman gives us the scoop on how he netted his job.

Tea-shop owner pours out wisdom on catering for her thirsty customers.

Ninjago City's biggest rock star chats about life in the music industry.

~~The Red Ninja rules!~~

GET LOST GARMABOY!!!

Signed, everyone.

SCHOOL RULES

NO vehicles on school grounds. Riding motorcycles in the corridors is not allowed.

NO headphones in class. Please enjoy your music at lunchtime. Loud noise disrupts others.

NO running while inside the school. The only exception is when the city is under attack.

Ninjago High star pupil

Everyone raise a cheer for Zane. He scored 100% in our "Beat the Computer" maths challenge. The computer only scored 99.5%.

NICE SUSHI YOU!

Part-time staff required in your favourite local sushi shop. Delivery drivers, chefs and cleaners, please apply in store!

ORDER YOUR SCHOOL PHOTO TODAY

VOLCANO LAIR

Lord Garmadon's volcano lair is more than a home – it's an office, a boardroom and a military headquarters too. From the outside, the cone-shaped volcano looks mysterious as it rises from the sea. Only a few wisps of smoke hint at the hotbed of activity within.

Tea stays hot forever in this lava-fuelled tea urn.

Volcano lair decorative features

Natural lighting
Flickering flames are *so* flattering to a tyrant's complexion.

Central heating
No fuel bills to pay here... heating's on the house (or in it).

Unpadded seats
A litte discomfort stops soldiers from nodding off during long speeches.

Home is where the heat is

Lord Garmadon enjoys a luxury volcanic lifestyle. Each morning starts with a piping hot breakfast in his nice warm bed. Only his custom volcano-print silk pyjamas keep him looking and feeling cool.

Volcano dress code

Garmadon likes a tidy-looking team. Soldiers wear dress uniforms with sashes for meetings. Nerds wear clean, white lab coats. Casual clothes are meant to be hidden, but many nerds risk unbuttoning their coats to cope with the heat.

Did you know?

Every vessel in Lord Garmadon's Shark Army has its own spot in a huge garage inside the volcano. From there, they can launch directly into the ocean.

GENERAL #1

Fired when no longer required

General #1 is the top-ranking officer in the Shark Army. He enjoys glory, power and a chance to bask in Lord Garmadon's evil shadow. There's just one snag. If he upsets his boss, he will be fired. From a volcano. Just like every other General #1 before him.

Wait, sir! I was only trying to help!

Large blaster to intimidate lower-ranking soldiers.

Military decorations

It's taken General #1 a long time to climb the ranks, and he's won a lot of medals along the way. He has an anchor medal, a shark medal and one that looks like a jellyfish. Who knows what grim things he has had to do to earn these rewards?

Did you know?

Lord Garmadon offers the position of General #1 to his son Lloyd. All Lloyd wants is for Garmadon to be a better father though, not his boss.

Easy ways to get fired

Let Garmadon's soda go flat
He likes the tongue-tingling taste of the bubbly drink.

Talk about your happy family life
He isn't happy. He has no family. Got it?

Be the perfect employee
Even if you do everything right, the boss might just get bored one day.

Out with the old

Being fired is humiliating. First, two oafs in octopus helmets drag you away. Then you're bundled into position and launched out of the volcano and into the sky. Then... whoa! Where do all these generals land anyway?

Silver shoulder guard is scratched from past battles.

Shiny #1 medal may soon be taken away from the General.

Fruit cocktail has an aftertaste of volcanic lava.

Thin, blue fins surround General #2's head, back and legs.

Fishy scale pattern can be seen under fins.

In with the new

When a General #1 is fired, the next-in-rank takes their place. This General #2 can't wait for her promotion. She hopes she won't upset Lord Garmadon. Nobody told her he can't stand to see officers slurping drinks on duty.

GARMA MECHA MAN

Lord Garmadon's nerds have designed a mech so huge and so scary that it is sure to have the ninja on the run. It's the Garma Mecha Man! The IT guys are proud of its fearsome features but the boss still has a few suggestions of his own to add. Suggestions? Make that demands.

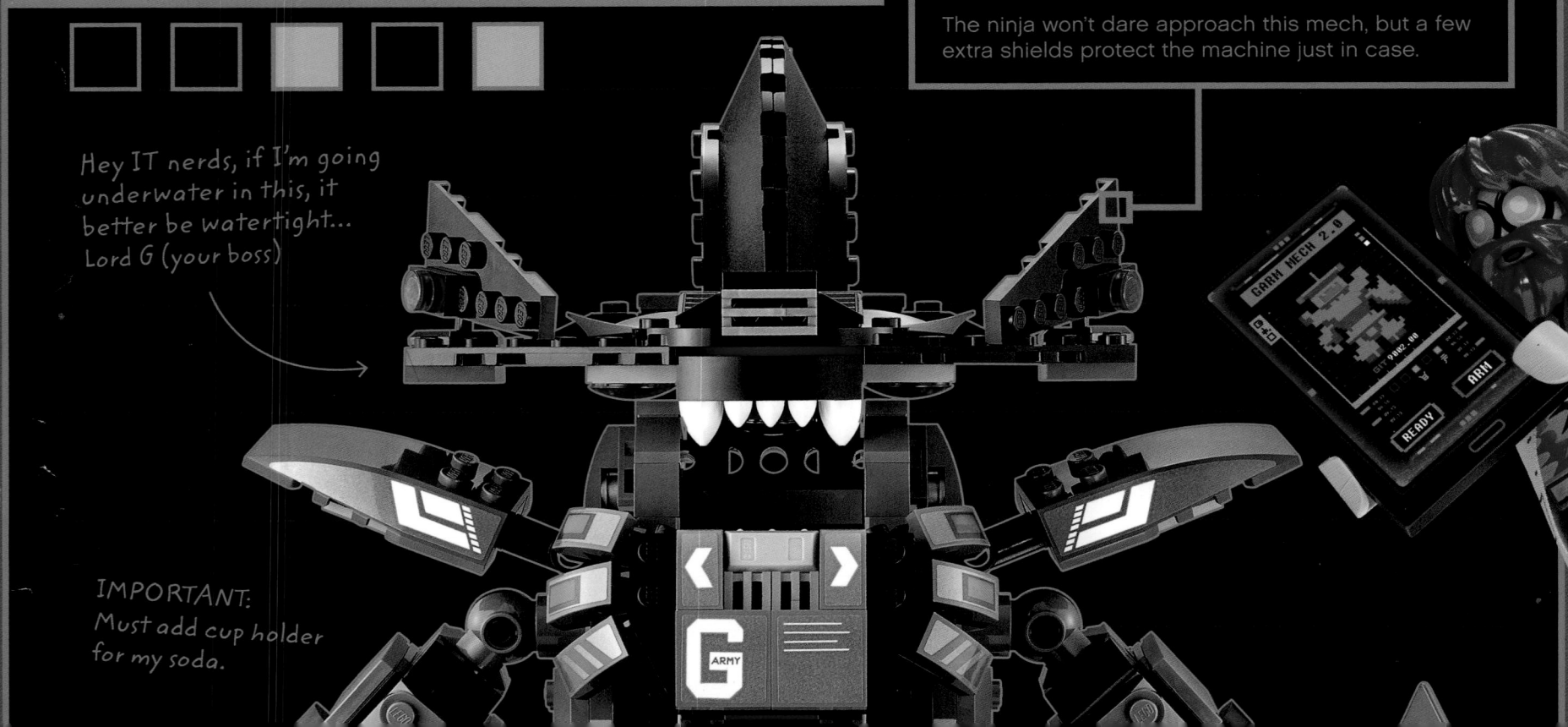

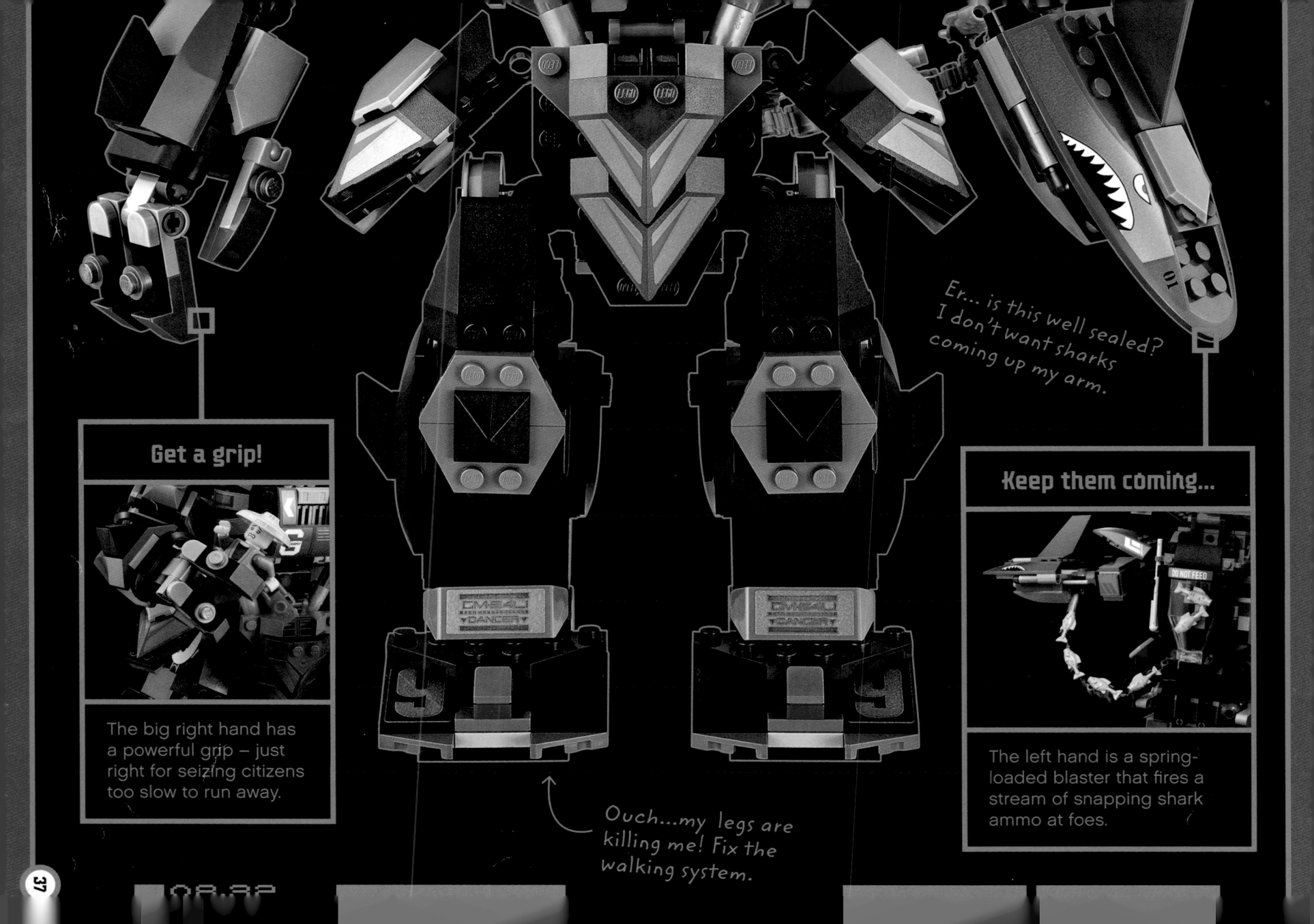
Er... is this well sealed? I don't want sharks coming up my arm.
Get a grip!
The big right hand has a powerful grip – just right for seizing citizens too slow to run away.
Keep them coming...
DO NOT FEED
The left hand is a spring-loaded blaster that fires a stream of snapping shark ammo at foes.
Ouch...my legs are killing me! Fix the walking system.

MASTER WU

Training up a new generation of ninja

Wise old Master Wu is training the Secret Ninja Force. It isn't easy. His pupils have not yet grasped that a true ninja relies on what is within, not just on technology. This has given Wu many headaches. Just as well he is an expert in the ninja art of staying calm!

Know the Ninjago language

The name "Wu" is written with two Ninjago language symbols. When written downwards, they look like a person wearing a hat!

Staff is used for fighting, resting on and helping with balance.

Weapon rack holds two staffs with tips shaped like hands.

Down in the dojo

Ninja training takes place on Master Wu's boat, *Destiny's Bounty*. The training area is called the dojo. Behind it is a wall with a scroll bearing Master Wu's symbol. Wu put the sign there to help the ninja focus their attention.

Ultimate secret

Master Wu is in possession of the Ultimate Weapon, which could help save Ninjago City from Lord Garmadon. He tries to keep it out of sight of the novice ninja. He worries they do not have the inner skills needed to control it.

Wu wear

Modern trends are not for Master Wu. He always wears traditional robes in calming, neutral colours. His robe even has a symbol meaning "peace" on the back. Wu's weapon is a low-tech but high-impact wooden staff.

Wu's best ways to stay balanced

Drink tea
Sip your tensions away with a relaxing cup of tea. Ahhhhh...

Play the flute
Soothe yourself with the sweet sound of traditional music.

Meditate
Sit down, close your eyes, breathe deep and let your mind come to rest.

WARRING WISDOM

The ninja often wish Master Wu's words of wisdom were easier to understand. They are even more confused when Lord Garmadon starts giving them advice, too. The brothers have opposite opinions, but which is the right way for the ninja?

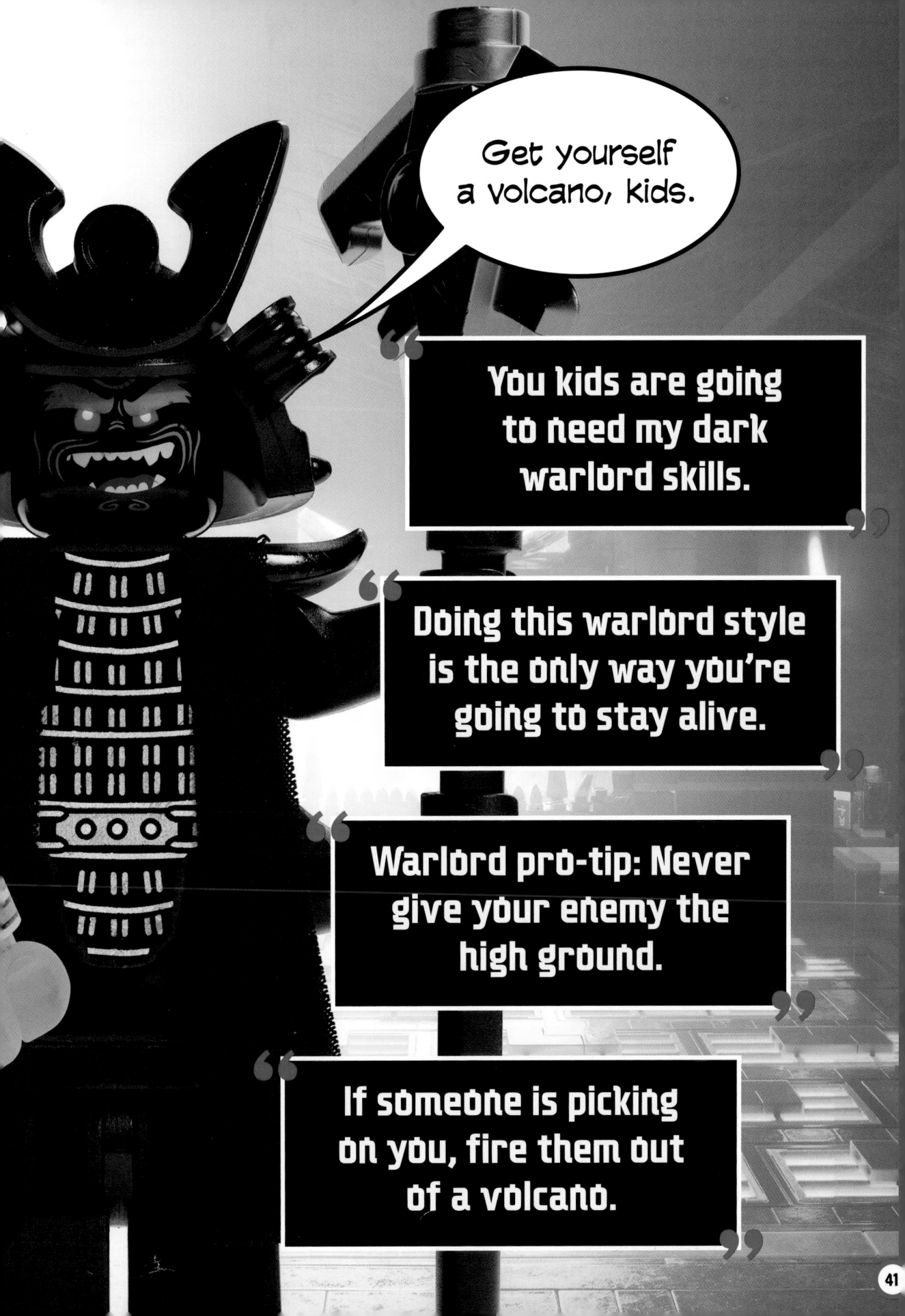
Get yourself a volcano, kids.
You kids are going to need my dark warlord skills.
Doing this warlord style is the only way you're going to stay alive.
Warlord pro-tip: Never give your enemy the high ground.
If someone is picking on you, fire them out of a volcano.

DESTINY'S BOUNTY

Master Wu's boat is moored at the docks in Ninjago City. Its name is *Destiny's Bounty*. The quaint old boat is decked out with jaunty lanterns, flags and plants. It does not look like a place where a ninja master would live and teach. But that's exactly what it is!

Hidden treasures

Ninja training weapons, such as the Green Ninja's sword, are stored in the dojo. But there are other weapons hidden under the deck, too. They include gold and silver katana swords, sharp sais and spiky shurikens.

Lessons on the water

A safe haven for all the ninja, *Destiny's Bounty* provides the team with a place to practise, relax, and spend time together. It is even a peaceful fishing spot!

Home sweet boat

When he isn't teaching, Master Wu retires to his living quarters at the back of the boat. Clever storage enables him to fit a lot into this small space. There is room for cooking, washing, meditating and sleeping.

Did you know?

Destiny's Bounty has two anchors. Both can be wound up and then dropped to stop the boat suddenly if it should start to drift.

Bumpers on boat stop the hull bashing against the dock walls.

COLE

He's strong, but not exactly silent

Cole is proud to be the strongest ninja and hones his body with vigorous daily workouts. He's a ninja of few words, but his cool, calm presence lets the others know he is right beside them in times of trouble. Well, that and the loud music he plays.

Beat to the beat!

The cockpit of Cole's mech has a record deck. When DJ Cole spins a disc, loud rock tunes blast from the speakers, creating shockwaves that can floor enemies. When Cole turns up the bass, he puts foes in their place!

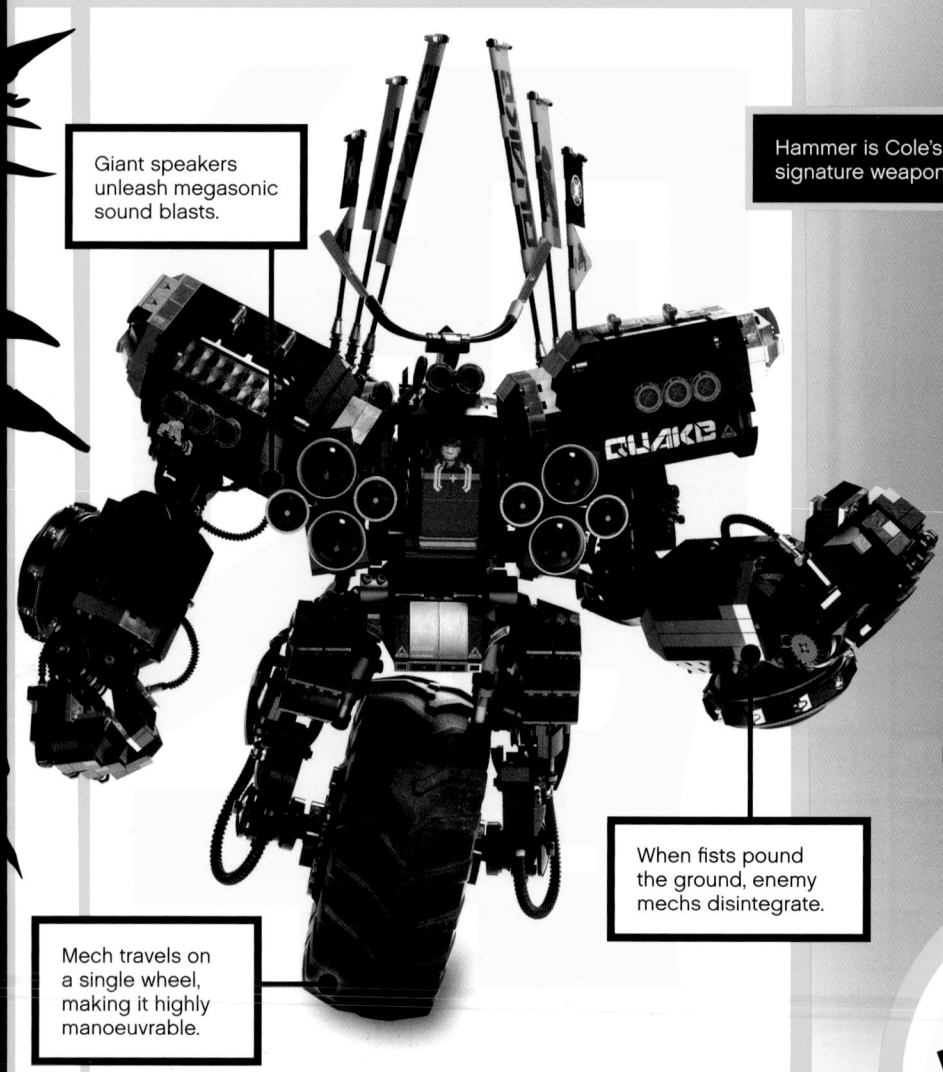

Giant speakers unleash megasonic sound blasts.

Hammer is Cole's signature weapon.

When fists pound the ground, enemy mechs disintegrate.

Mech travels on a single wheel, making it highly manoeuvrable.

Cole's Quake Mech

Cole likes his rock music heavy and his mech to match. The massive machine has hefty, ground-pounding fists and broad shoulders fitted with giant speakers. Even the single wheel is oversized – and it needs to be to support all that weighty tech up top.

Know the Ninjago language

Small print on the arm of Cole's mech carries a Ninjago language warning about "dangerous vibrations".

We are all so ninja!

Sleeveless top shows off Cole's strong biceps.

Distractions from training

Listening to music
At school, in the dojo or in battle, Cole usually has his headphones on.

Making music
Cole lays down his own tracks, each perfectly mixed to knock out his foes.

Styling his man-bun
He never forgets to take a selfie to show off when his hair looks so ninja!

Down to earth ninja

This trusty ninja is very grounded, so it is no wonder he is the Ninja of Earth. Cole wears clothes in dark, earthy shades and fights with a hammer. A lightweight, sleeveless top keeps Cole as cool as he thinks he is.

MY SECRET DIARY

It hurts my feelings when people are mean to me because of who my dad is. I told Master Wu, and he suggested I write everything down in this diary, good and bad. It helps me to remember that although people tease Lloyd, they really, really love the Green Ninja... and that's me, too!

7am

Uhhh... not feeling so bright this morning. Another sleepless night wondering what to do about my dad, Garmadon.

7:30 am

I wish Mum wouldn't turn the TV on at breakfast. There's usually something bad on about Dad. I've lost my appetite.

DON'T FORGET
- Homework
- Save the city
- Unblock the fire hose on Kai's mech.

8am

Here we go... get on the school bus, smile, say hello, find a seat. Ignore it when everyone moves to the other side of the bus.

8:30 am

Arrive at school. Wipe off the "Garmadork" graffiti scrawled on my locker and head off to my classroom. At least Cole, Jay, Nya, Kai and Zane are here.

PROPERTY OF LLOYD GARMADON

2 pm

Dad's on the attack... time to save the city again! I feel better now I'm the Green Ninja, I'm in my Dragon Mech and everyone's cheering me. Wonder how those upgrades are gonna perform?

5 pm

Dad called. What could he possibly want to talk about? It turns out he didn't even mean to call me – it was just an accident.

7 pm

Yay! Time to chill with my buddies. We talk about today's battle and how awesomely ninja we all are. They don't care who my dad is. I love these guys. I love being a ninja!

SO NINJA!

DO NOT READ!!

CITY BATTLE

Battle is raging in Ninjago City – and it's the worst battle yet! The ninja mechs cannot hold back the dreaded Garma Mecha Man, and it looks as though the city will fall to Lord Garmadon at last. Could things possibly get any worse?

Did you know?

Lord Garmadon heads for the tallest spot in Ninjago City – the Great Tower. He wants to plant a conquering flag there, to mark his victory.

Scarier than sharks!

The Shark Army streams through the streets, leaving a trail of destruction. They are about to learn that something even more destructive is coming. A beast is in the city – and the city might not be a very safe place for a fish!

Blow by blow

Disobeying orders

Lloyd is desperate not to let his dad win this battle. He disobeys Master Wu and tries to use the Ultimate Weapon on Garmadon. It doesn't work quite how Lloyd expects!

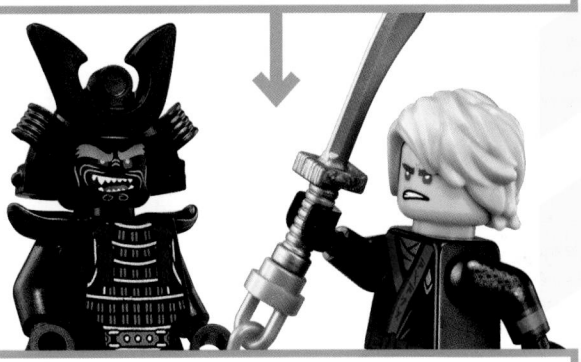

I wish you weren't my father!

Lord Garmadon gloats over Lloyd's failure, prompting Lloyd to angrily reveal his true identity. He utters the devastating words, "I wish you weren't my father!"

Beast on the loose

While Garmadon reels at Lloyd's words, a beast summoned by the Ultimate Weapon rampages through the city. Citizens flee as buildings crash down all around them.

KAI

Hothead who's hot on the battlefield

Kai is always rushing into things and taking crazy risks. He says he's bold – others say he's reckless! He must learn that when he puts himself in danger, he puts the team in danger too. He might even be putting that well-styled hair of his in danger. Whoah!

The heat is off

When the battle is over (and hopefully won), it's time to chill. Kai and his teammates head back to the Mech Garage to relax and unwind. Kai's mech-sized recliner chair is a welcome sight for a worn-out ninja.

Icon on flag contains the Ninjago language symbols for "Kai".

Fire blasters shoot flames from the mech's hands.

Monumental mech

Glossy, red and terrifyingly tall, Kai's Fire Mech can scorch a path through enemy lines in no time. Disc shooters on its shoulders take out far-off foes, while fire blasters on the arms melt enemy mechs that dare to get too close.

Kai's favourite conversation topics

The Red Ninja
Kai loves to recount stories of his daring moves in battle.

Red Ninja fans
Kai is always looking out for Red Ninja fans in crowds of cheering citizens.

What's for dinner?
Croissants, sushi or tacos, Kai loves trying new dishes.

In the red

Kai is very proud of his fiery red robes and twin katana swords. They are important parts of being a member of the Secret Ninja Force. Being seen with scratches, scars or plasters doesn't seem to bother Kai though. Maybe he thinks they make him look dashing!

PERILOUS JOURNEY

What is more powerful than the Ultimate Weapon? The Ultimate Ultimate Weapon, of course! It could save Ninjago City, but to find it the ninja must make a long and perilous journey across Ninjago Island. Master Wu is not sure they have what it takes, but the ninja want to try. Onward, ninja!

...and climb to the top of a shaky, quaky temple!
Temple guard dogs
Temple of the Ultimate Ultimate Weapon
...pass over tall, cloud-shrouded mountains...
Master Falls
...cross turbulent waters and battle weird, wild foes...

THE JUNGLE

Welcome to the jungle – the deep, dense, Ninjago jungle. The ninja are here in search of the Ultimate Ultimate Weapon that could help save their city. But in this weird, wild place and with no mechs to rely on, they're way out of their comfort zone.

Farewell, Ninjago City

The ninja have no choice but to enter the scary jungle to fulfil their mission. Before they do, they turn and wave goodbye to their beloved city. They wave goodbye to their mechs, gadgets and technology too. Oh dear!

Did you know?

The Ninjago jungle is known by some as the "Forest of Whispers". Master Wu has excellent hearing but the ninja must learn how to listen to the natural world.

There's quite a drop at this end of the bridge. Watch out!

Danger everywhere!

There's lots to watch out for in the jungle. Wild animals. Poisonous plants. Bandits. Rickety bridges. Maybe even Lord Garmadon, desperate to get his hands on the Ultimate Ultimate Weapon before the ninja can.

Jungle master

Master Wu is quite at home in the jungle. In tune with nature, he can sense danger as it approaches. Wu knows that the ninja must master this skill too, but it is a lesson they must learn on their own.

ZANE

Robot ninja who's always chilled

Who is the coolest ninja of all? That's Zane, the Ninja of Ice. This archer is a robot, a video player and a walking calculator. He's a good pal too, offering "friendly companionship mode" to his teammates in good times or bad.

Know the Ninjago language

The Ice Mech features a clue to its owner's identity. A sign near the cockpit features symbols meaning "Zane".

Only human

Zane would love to experience life as a normal teen. His robot sensors help him to copy human behaviour, but sometimes misfire. It's awkward when you realise you laughed at something that wasn't a joke.

Cool guy; hot shot! Zane's bow fires freezing arrows at foes.

Ice Tank

Zane scores many crushing victories in his Ice Tank, thanks to its giant, mech-mashing tracks. A rotating container at the back provides its rapid shooter with a steady supply of icy ammo to freeze foes as they flee.

Ice cannon has a six-stud rapid shooter.

Tracks crush enemy mechs like a mallet crushes ice.

White-clad warrior

Washing powder must top Zane's shopping list. His white costume is simply spotless! Zane's weapon is a bow and arrow. With the robot ability to control speed and trajectory, this awesome archer always hits his mark.

Zane's special robot skills

Recognising emotions
Programming enables him to tell smiles from snarls.

Keeping quiet
Zane switches on "silent mode" when Master Wu asks for quiet in the dojo.

Instant calculations
Can be offputting when he calculates ninja chances of success as "zero".

TEMPLE

Deep in the jungle stands the ancient Temple of the Ultimate Ultimate Weapon. It contains a glorious prize, but it also contains many hazards. Will the ninja find what they are looking for inside its walls? If they do, will they make it out again?

Guard dogs

Two fearsome stone dogs guard the temple. These horrible hounds are trained to scare off intruders. Few people are brave enough to discover that they can be easily tamed with a tickle on the tummy!

Ancient Ninjago features such as roof carvings are rare in the city.

Temple traps

Finding the jungle temple is tricky enough. Getting to the top is even trickier. The ninja must dodge a trapdoor, rock dropper, dynamite dropper, blade shooters, sword trap and hanging cage along the way.

Did you know?

Master Wu warned his students about the Temple of Fragile Foundations. The ninja better watch their step as they explore.

Wall art gives clues about the temple's former residents.
Lloyd searches everywhere for the Ultimate Ultimate Weapon.
The library contains an old, mysterious scroll.

LESSONS FROM THE JUNGLE

For city kids like the ninja, the jungle is a strange and unfamiliar place. They will have to learn some lessons quickly – and that's just to survive, let alone to fulfil their mission. Come to think of it, the jungle holds a few important lessons for those who have been here before, too.

Nya
I've learned to be less competitive. Getting through the jungle together safely was all that mattered. Wu's lessons were key to keeping us all safe.

Kai
I've learned to keep quiet – sometimes for even more than thirty seconds! You never know when a listening enemy is hiding in the undergrowth, so stealth is vital.

Cole
The sounds of the jungle can tell you a lot about who and what is around you. I've learned to take my headphones off and replace them with a cunning disguise.

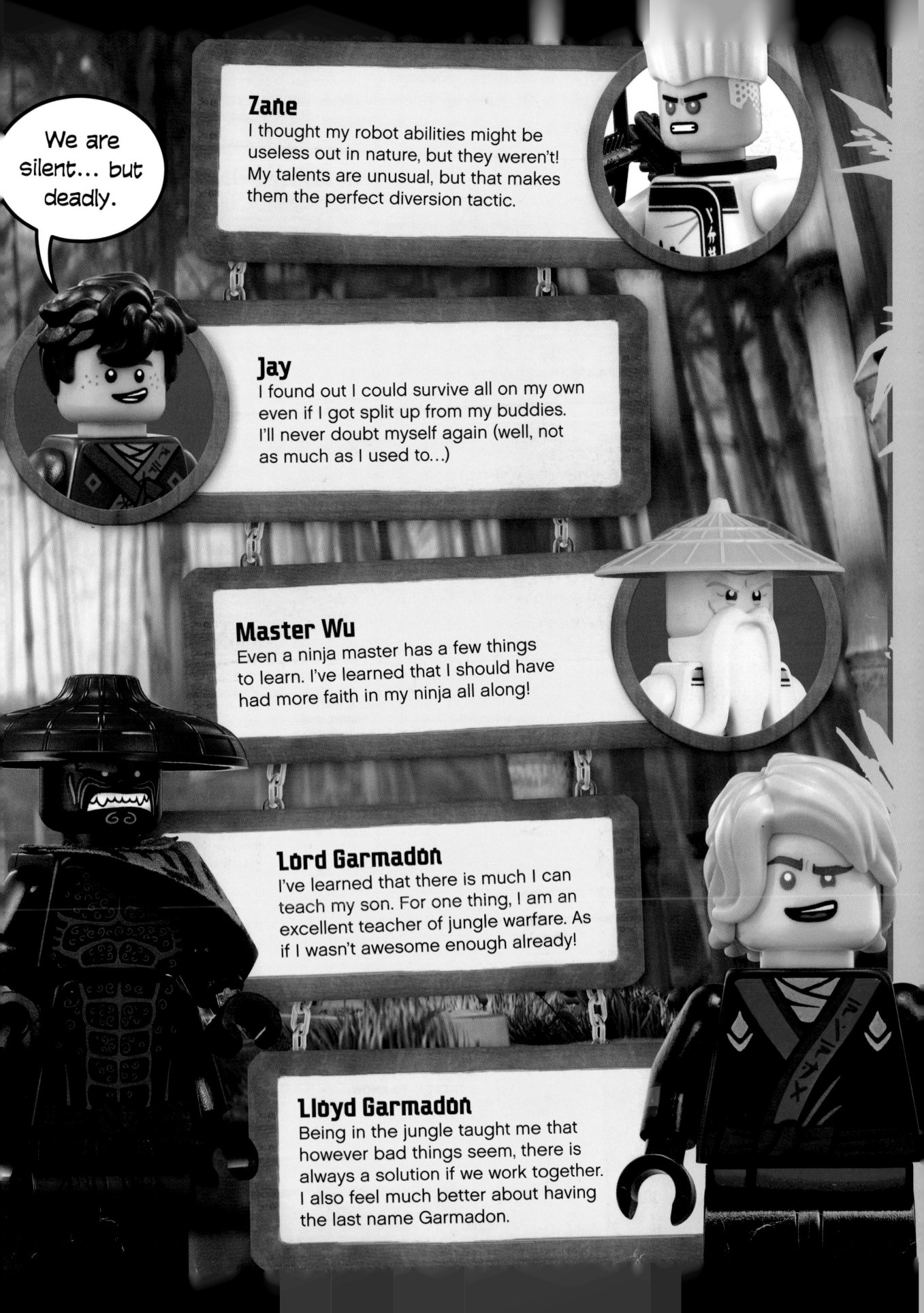

Zane

I thought my robot abilities might be useless out in nature, but they weren't! My talents are unusual, but that makes them the perfect diversion tactic.

Jay

I found out I could survive all on my own even if I got split up from my buddies. I'll never doubt myself again (well, not as much as I used to...)

Master Wu

Even a ninja master has a few things to learn. I've learned that I should have had more faith in my ninja all along!

Lord Garmadon

I've learned that there is much I can teach my son. For one thing, I am an excellent teacher of jungle warfare. As if I wasn't awesome enough already!

Lloyd Garmadon

Being in the jungle taught me that however bad things seem, there is always a solution if we work together. I also feel much better about having the last name Garmadon.

ACKNOWLEDGEMENTS

Editor Beth Davies
Designer Sam Bartlett
Pre-Production Producers Siu Yin Chan and Jennifer Murray
Producer Louise Daly
Managing Editor Paula Regan
Design Manager Jo Connor
Art Director Lisa Lanzarini
Publisher Julie Ferris
Publishing Director Simon Beecroft

DK would like to thank Randi Sørensen, Paul Hansford, Martin Leighton Lindhardt, Heidi K. Jensen and Simon Lucas at the LEGO Group; Ben Harper at Warner Bros.; and Emma Grange and Jenny Edwards at DK for editorial and design assistance.

First published in Great Britain in 2017
by Dorling Kindersley Limited
80 Strand, London WC2R 0RL
A Penguin Random House Company

10 9 8 7 6 5 4 3 2 1
001–280784–August/2017

J 791.4372 MARCH

March, Julia.
LEGO, the ninjago movie

R0172027532 M_KING

Atlanta-Fulton Public Library